YOUR
NEW LIFE

By

Duane Vander Klok

All scripture quotations are from the
New King James Version
unless otherwise indicated.

YOUR NEW LIFE

published by Resurection Life Church
5100 Ivanrest Ave. S.W.
Grandville, MI 49418
616-534-4923

ISBN 978-0-9798642-2-3
Library of Congress catalog card number: 2001098332

Printed in the United States of America

CONTENTS

INTRODUCTION

Asking Jesus to be your Savior is only the beginning of the Christian life. He wants to be your Lord, too. The promises and blessings God has for you are waiting to be claimed; but you can't claim and experience them if you don't know about them. The good news is that when you know how to receive what God has for you, the devil won't be able to keep you miserable, lonely, or depressed.

Each chapter describes an area where God wants you to experience freedom as you learn to walk with Him each day. Now that you have been born again, it's time to discover what YOUR NEW LIFE is all about!

Chapter 1

A NEW CREATION
IN CHRIST

YOUR NEW LIFE

Something happens to you on the inside when you receive Jesus. To fully understand this, you need to know what happened in the Garden of Eden. Genesis 3 tells the story of how God told Adam and Eve not to eat the fruit of the Tree of the Knowledge of Good and Evil. If they did, God warned them, on that day they would die. Unfortunately, in spite of the warning, they disobeyed and ate from the tree. They didn't drop dead physically, but a part of them *did* die—that part that has fellowship with God. Adam and Eve couldn't understand or talk with God like before. In fact, they were afraid of Him and hid from Him. When you receive Jesus Christ as Lord of your life, He takes that dead part of your spirit and makes you alive toward Him again. You become a brand new person on the inside.

To help us understand our new life, let's look at a story Jesus once told in Luke 16:19-23 about a rich man and a beggar.

"There was a certain rich man who was clothed in purple and fine linen and fared sumptuously every day. But there was a certain beggar named Lazarus, full of sores, who was laid at his gate, desiring to be fed with the crumbs which fell from the rich man's table. Moreover the dogs came and licked his sores. So it was that the beggar died, and was carried

by the angels to Abraham's bosom. The rich man also died and was buried. And being in torment in Hades, he lifted up his eyes and saw Abraham afar off, and Lazarus in his bosom."

Notice that when the beggar died, he was *"carried by the angels."* What did they carry? Not his body because it was buried in the ground, probably in a pauper's tomb. They carried his spirit. You see, the real you lives on the inside of your body. The real you is your spirit.

1 Thessalonians 5:23 says,

"Now may the God of peace Himself sanctify you completely; and may your whole spirit, soul, and body be preserved blameless at the coming of our Lord Jesus Christ."

You are a three-part being—body, soul, and spirit. Your spirit is the part of you . . .

- . . . that has fellowship with God;
- . . . that worships and contacts the spiritual realm;
- . . . that is who you really are;
- . . . that becomes brand new when you receive Jesus;
- . . . that will live forever and ever.

YOUR NEW LIFE

The above scripture tells us that we also have a soul—that is your mind. (When God breathed into Adam, he became a living soul.) The soul, because it is linked with the spirit, will also live forever. The soul part of man contacts the intellectual realm and includes the emotions, the will, and the intellect. A college education does not change who you are. Even before you could read or write, you were still "you." In fact, no matter how much you educate your intellect, it doesn't change who you are because you are not a mind; you are a spirit.

The third part of your being is your body, the part your spirit lives in. James 2:26 says, *"For as the body without the spirit is dead, so faith without works is dead also."* (Death is when your spirit steps out of your body.) When you received Jesus, He makes your spirit new. You didn't get a new body or a new mind, which is why you need to do something about your mind after you are saved. Romans 12:2 says,

"Do not be conformed to this world, but be transformed by the renewing of your mind, that you may prove what is that good and acceptable and perfect will of God."

Therefore, after you are saved, you need to change the way you think. You do that by reading and meditating on the Word of God.

When you have an idea, a thought, or a moral that is different than what the Word says, take that thought, throw it away and receive God's thought on the matter. The Bible contains God's thoughts and ideas on every subject.

When you got saved, God gave you a new spirit on the inside, and now you have

Your mind needs to be trained to think the kind of thoughts that bless you rather than destroy you.

fellowship with Him. But *you* are the one who must do something about your mind. I can't emphasize enough the importance of this! God did something with your spirit, but *you* must do something with your mind and body. Your mind needs to be trained to think the kind of thoughts that bless you rather than destroy you.

As for your third part, your body, it didn't change when you got saved either. In fact, Romans 7:23 says,

"But I see another law <u>in my members</u>, warring against the law of my mind, and bringing me into captivity to the law of sin which is <u>in my members</u>."

"In my members" means "in my body." Your body (your flesh) will still want to do wrong things even though you are a Christian because your body did not get saved. But your spirit, the part that has God's life in it, will never

want to do anything against God, His Word or His will. So your spirit is never going to agree to sin. The Bible says,

> *"Whoever has been born of God does not sin, for His seed remains in him; and he cannot sin, because he has been born of God"*

(1 John 3:9).

The Amplified Bible puts it this way, *"No one born [begotten] of God [deliberately and knowingly] habitually practices sin."* Because your new spirit will never agree to sin, you now face the challenge of keeping your flesh from dominating your life with its selfish demands: *"I want* to eat this; *I want* to do this; *I want* to go there!" Your spirit, where the life of God now resides, must dominate your life.

Can you see why you need to understand your new life in Christ? Without this understanding, you won't know what to do when your selfish flesh wants to continue telling you what to do. Sometimes newly saved Christians, not realizing

Without this understanding, you won't know what to do when your selfish flesh wants to continue telling you what to do.

they must now deliberately choose to obey their spirit, get confused about the inner battle that follows their salvation. So they give up; and, even though they are saved, they walk under the control of their flesh and are miserable. God, however, wants you to experience the joy and freedom of being led by the spirit instead of by the selfish flesh. He wants your spirit to dominate your life so those addictions of the flesh can't control you any more. That's why God made you new inside. That's why He put His very life and nature inside of you. He loves you and has done everything He could to set you free from the devil's grasp. You need to know and understand your new life so you can experience the victories and the joys that God has for you. You *can* walk in the spirit and not fulfill the lusts of your flesh. Remember:

1) Your spirit is saved and has God's life and nature in it.
2) Your mind must be renewed by changing the way you think. You do that by meditating on God's Word (Romans 12:2).
3) Your body did not get saved, and you must take authority over it by listening to and obeying your spirit (Romans 12:1).

Chapter 2

WATER
BAPTISM

YOUR NEW LIFE

Some of us were brought up in denominations where we were baptized as little children. But the Bible tells us to repent, believe and be baptized. When we are babies, only a few months old, we are not able to repent or believe. In Acts 2 the people asked, *"What must we do to be saved?"* Peter told them, *"Repent and be baptized in the name of Jesus for the remission of sins."* We are to be baptized after we have repented and made Jesus the Lord of our life.

Someone might ask, "Why should I get baptized?" First of all, we should get baptized as an act of obedience. In Matthew 28:19-20, Jesus Himself commanded the disciples to baptize believers:

> *"Go therefore and make disciples of all the nations, baptizing them in the name of the Father and of the Son and of the Holy Spirit, teaching them to observe all things that I have commanded you; and lo, I am with you always, even to the end of the age."*

Second, baptism is identifying with Jesus' death, burial, and resurrection. When you get saved, you become a new person on the inside, a new person in Christ. The Bible says in 2 Corinthians 5:17 that *"old things have passed away."* That means the old person you used to be is dead. Paul put it this way, *"My old man was crucified with Christ."* When someone dies, you bury the "old man"—the dead body. That's also what happens when a person gets water baptized. You are taking the "old you" and "burying" it in a watery grave.

Romans 6:3-4 tells us what happens when we get baptized.

> *"Do you not know that as many of us as were baptized into Christ Jesus were baptized into his death? Therefore, we were buried with him through baptism into death, that just as Christ was raised from the dead by the glory of the Father, even so we also should walk in newness of life."*

When you are baptized, you are agreeing to receive what Jesus did for you. As you come up out of that water, you are announcing to the world, "I am going to live a new life." Any past sins or condemnation, any shame or reproach

> *When you are baptized, you are agreeing to receive what Jesus did for you.*

in your life is left behind in that watery grave, and you come up to live a brand new life.

In Colossians 2:11-12 (WT), this explanation is given:

YOUR NEW LIFE

"In Him also you were circumcised with a circumcision not performed by hand, when you threw off your sinful nature in true Christian circumcision; having been buried with Him in your baptism, in which you were also raised with Him through faith produced within you by God who raised him from among the dead."

It may seem hard to understand, but when you get water baptized, God says he will cut (circumcise) the hardness, the criticalness, and the bondage out of your heart so that you come up out of the water with a brand new heart announcing to all that you will live a brand new life.

If you have not been water baptized, I want to encourage you to do so as soon as you possibly can! I have known people who have been Christians for years who were unable to get free from certain things in their lives—such as certain habits and addictions—but once they were baptized, they experienced freedom as God circumcised their hearts in their obedience to the act of baptism.

Chapter 3

FRIENDS

YOUR NEW LIFE

Few of us realize how deeply friends affect us, yet they have a very profound influence on our lives. They affect our morals, our values—even how we handle anger and bitterness. Taking the counsel of an ungodly friend can be devastating. That's why the Bible warns us to choose our friends carefully. *"The righteous should choose his friends carefully, for the way of the wicked leads them astray"* (Proverbs 12:26).

Did you know it is impossible to have a close friendship with an ungodly person without being affected by them? 1 Corinthians 15:33 clearly states this truth: *"Don't be deceived, 'Evil company corrupts good habits.'"* It's like a promise—bad friends *will* corrupt you. In fact, if your new life begins to unravel in areas such as marriage, money, job, anger, or addictions, check the type of friends you are hanging around with. You will almost always find the root of many of your problems is the type of friends you are keeping. I have heard Proverbs 13:20 paraphrased this way: *"He who walks with wise men will stack up wisdom, but for the one who is a companion of fools, his life will begin to unravel."* Because it is easy to pick up their habits or ways of thinking, it's no wonder your life has started to unravel. There is a Bible story in 2

> You will almost always find the root of many of your problems is the type of friends you are keeping.

Samuel 13:1-5 (LB) that vividly illustrates how a bad friendship can affect a person.

> *"Prince Absalom, David's son, had a beautiful sister named Tamar. And Prince Amnon (her half brother) fell desperately in love with her. Amnon became so tormented by his love for her that he became ill. He had no way of talking to her, for the girls and young men were kept strictly apart. But Amnon had a very crafty friend—his cousin, Jonadab (the son of David's brother, Shime-ah). One day Jonadab said to Amnon, 'What's the trouble? Why should the son of a king look so haggard morning after morning?'*
>
> *So Amnon told him, 'I am in love with Tamar, my half sister.'*
>
> *'Well,' Jonadab said, 'I'll tell you what to do. Go back to bed and pretend you are sick; when your father comes to see you, ask him to let Tamar come and prepare some food for you. Tell him you'll feel better if she feeds you.'*

Friends are a powerful influence for good or bad.

Amnon listened to his friend's advice and used the opportunity to rape his sister. Later Tamar's brother killed

Amnon for what he did to his sister. Friends are a powerful influence for good or bad. *"He who walks with wise men will be wise, but the companion of fools will be destroyed"* (Proverbs 13:20).

After asking Jesus into your heart, you will probably find that you aren't comfortable with your old friendships anymore because you no longer value the same things. Let those relationships die. The Bible says, *"Can two walk together unless they are agreed?"* (Amos 3:3). Make new friends with godly, wise people who will encourage and support your new life.

During the time when you are making new friends, you may be tempted to get discouraged. That's normal, but don't worry. God will bring new relationships into your life that will bless and strengthen you. Personally, I lost almost every friend I had because our values and interests were now different. I was interested in Bible study, pleasing God, and worship, and they were not. God brought new friends into my life as I asked Him to. I believe He will do the same for you if you ask Him.

Chapter 4

RENEWING
YOUR MIND

YOUR NEW LIFE

In baptism, God miraculously deals with your heart, removing your past and the hardness of your heart, but then you must patiently deal with your mind. *"Do not be conformed to this world,"* God says in Romans 12:2,*"but be transformed by the renewing of your mind, that you may prove what is that good and acceptable and perfect will of God."*

> A dirty mouth and a bitter attitude are not just sins—they are also habits. God deals with the sin, but you must deal with the habit.

A dirty mouth and a bitter attitude are not just sins—they are also habits. God deals with the sin, but you must deal with the habit. That's why it is important after salvation and baptism to renew your mind. God tells us to *"lay aside all filthiness and overflow of wickedness, and receive with meekness the implanted word, which is able to save your souls"* (James 1:21). That means you need to replace your old way of thinking with God's way of thinking. So He shows you what He thinks in His Word.

As you read and meditate on His Word, you will find a wonderful confidence and faith rising in your heart. That's because *"faith comes by hearing, and hearing by the Word of God"* Romans 10:17. You will also discover that renewing your mind with the Truth has now given you a choice—my way or God's way? Lies and deception and bitterness won't appeal to you any more. Right choices will be easier to make. Instead of making choices based on your feelings, on your past or on deceptions, you now have the strength and faith to make right choices based on the Truth. The Word is now your standard rather than your shifting, deceptive feelings or circumstances. *"Therefore all your precepts concerning all things I consider to be right. I hate every false way"* (Psalms 119:128).

> Instead of making choices based on your feelings, on your past or on deceptions, you now have the strength and faith to make right choices based on the Truth.

Therefore, after you have been baptized, get involved in a Bible study and personal Bible reading. *"As newborn babes, desire the pure milk of the word, that you may grow thereby"* (1 Peter 2:2). If you want to grow and know God's will for every circumstance, then you must renew your mind!

Chapter 5

THE WORD OF GOD

YOUR NEW LIFE

No child is ever born full-grown. When you are born again spiritually, you are not spiritually full-grown either. Just as you have a need to grow physically, you also have a need to grow spiritually. Jesus said in Matthew 4:4, *"It is written, 'Man shall not live by bread alone, but by every word that proceeds from the mouth of God.'"* You feed your body physical food every day, and you need to feed your heart spiritual food—God's Word—every day so you can develop a strong, healthy spirit. *"Like newborn babies, crave pure spiritual milk, so that by it you may grow up in your salvation, now that you have tasted that the Lord is good"* (1 Peter 2:2, NIV).

You may want to start by reading three chapters every day. I recommend that you start in the New Testament because we're living the New Testament times. I would also recommend that you read it at the same time every day so it becomes a habit. I have a friend who doesn't like to read, so he bought the Bible on CD and listens to it in the car as he drives to work. For many people, listening to the Bible on an mp3 or CD player works very well.

Reading the Bible is like reading a letter God has written especially to you.

Most of the direction that God gives you is going to come to you through His Word. He will speak to you through His Word to reveal His will for your life. Therefore, reading the

Bible is like reading a letter God has written especially to you.

The Bible says the Spirit of God inspired every word in it.

> *"All Scripture is given by inspiration of God, and is profitable for doctrine, for reproof, for correction, for instruction in righteousness that the man of God may be complete, thoroughly equipped for every good work"*
>
> (2 Timothy 3:16).

If I pick up a book and read it, I am reading the thoughts of the person who wrote it. But when I pick up the Bible and read it, I am reading the

Whose thinking needs to change? God's or mine?

thoughts of God. Through His letter to you, God is preparing you for the special plan He has for your life. As you read it, He will teach and correct you. For example, when I am reading the Word of God, I might find it says something different than my opinion about marriage or money, or correcting my children, or premarital sex. Whose thinking needs to change? God's or mine? God's Word is the standard by which we judge all things. Every way or thought that disagrees with God will eventually bring harm into my life. That's why I need to reject any thought that disagrees with the Truth. God didn't give us "thou-shalt-not" commandments to keep us from enjoying life or because He is an ogre. He gave them because He loves us and wants to keep us from the harm that would come from those sins. He tells us not to do those things for our good, to protect us. Deuteronomy 10:13 says, *"and to keep the commandments of the Lord and His statutes which I command you today for your good?*

That's what God tells Joshua after Moses died. Joshua is about to fill Moses' shoes, which is a rather intimidating responsibility since Moses is the man who went up on the mountain and received the commandments directly from God Himself. He's the man who walked in the power of God and confronted the mighty Pharoah of Egypt with the ten plagues, then led the Hebrews to freedom by splitting the Red Sea. Joshua, about to follow in this guy's steps, was probably full of fear and trepidation. So God tells him,

"This Book of the Law shall not depart from your mouth, but you shall meditate in it day and night, that you may observe to do according to all that is written in it. For then you will make your way prosperous, and then you will have good success."

(Joshua 1:8).

God didn't want Joshua being intimidated by someone else's success, so He told him how to be successful himself. You see, God had a plan for Joshua's life, and He wanted Joshua to be prepared for it. Making God's Word the standard for your life will cause you, too, to prosper and succeed.

When God told Joshua to meditate on the Word, He meant for him to do more than just read it. The word *meditate* means "to think about, to talk about, to muse." It means to come at it from the north, south, east and west, thinking about it until you get everything out of it you can. Jesus said in Mark 4:24 (AMP),

> *"Be careful what you are hearing. The measure [of thought and study] you give [to the truth you hear] will be the measure [of virtue and knowledge] that comes back to you, and more [besides] will be given to you who hear."*

Just hearing the Word once is not enough. It is the thought and study, the thinking and praying about it that opens up the revelation of everything God wants to say to you personally in a particular verse of scripture.

Probably the best way I know how to explain meditation is to describe a cow. She goes out in the field and eats grass, then finds a shady spot where she lies down and regurgitates the food she has eaten. Then she chews it again. That is what meditation is like. You may read the Word of God or you may hear a message preached at church, but afterwards you need to think about it again, meditate on it more, muse on it, talk about it with others. As you do, you will receive revelation and insight into what you heard or read.

Something that will help you get more out of your Bible reading and study is to first ask God to open your spiritual eyes. Psalm 119:18 says, *"Open my eyes, that I may see wondrous things from your law."* He wants to give you everything you need to grow strong and healthy in your spirit and to know His will for your life. Ask Him to help you understand what you read. You will get far more out of it with His help.

Remember when you read the Bible your faith grows because *"faith comes by hearing, and hearing by the word of God"* (Romans 10:17). A person's spiritual growth will usually get misdirected if they don't read the Word of God.

Chapter 6

BELONGING TO A BODY OF BELIEVERS

YOUR NEW LIFE

Jesus had a great ministry while He was on earth, but that ministry is not over. He also has a present day ministry, and part of that ministry is building the church. Jesus referred to this in Matthew 16:18: *"And I also say to you that you are Peter, and on this rock I will build My church, and the gates of Hades shall not prevail against it."*

When you become a Christian, the Holy Spirit takes and puts (baptizes) you into the body of Christ (the Church). It is not God's will that you live your life as a Christian alone. He has made you a part of His family, His body, and He wants you to be involved in the church. Whatever God does in the earth today, He does through the church. As we participate in a local church, 1 Corinthians 3:9a (TEV) tells us that we *"are partners working together for God."*

Have you ever heard someone say, "I can be just as good a Christian at home as I can at church." That is not true. Actually, if you separate yourself from the body of believers, you are disobeying a number of scriptures. Proverbs 18:1 tells us, *"A man who isolates (separates) himself seeks his own desire. He rages against all wise judgment."* A believer who doesn't want to be part of a body of believers is one who wants to seek his own interests and do his own thing.

If you separate yourself from the body of believers, you are disobeying a number of scriptures.

BELONGING TO A BODY OF BELIEVERS

There is protection in fellowshipping with other believers. At our house we eat a lot of bananas. Do you know which banana gets eaten first? The first one that gets separated from the bunch. Spiritually the same thing happens when a person tries to stand alone. He is more susceptible to the works of the devil. 1 Peter 5:8 tells us to *"be sober, be vigilant; because your adversary the devil walks about like a roaring lion, seeking whom he may devour."* Can you guess who will be the first one to be devoured? The one who is standing alone, of course. Hebrews 10:25 urges us,

> *". . . not forsaking the assembling of ourselves together, as is the manner of some, but exhorting one another, and so much the more as you see the Day* [that is, when Jesus returns] *approaching."*

This is a direct command to fellowship together as believers. Actually, there are over thirty verses in the New Testament that a person obeys if he chooses to have fellowship in a group or church situation. For example, here are two:

- Hebrews 13:1 - *"but exhort one another daily while it is called "today," lest any of you be hardened through the deceitfulness of sin."*

- Hebrews 10:24 – *"And let us consider one another in order to stir up love and good works."*

So many of God's commands in the Bible are things we cannot do alone. Fifty-eight times we are told to do things to, for, and with "one another." We are to serve, help, pray for, put up with, encourage, love, forgive, and greet one another. You cannot obey these verses if you are isolated from other Christians.

There's another reason to find your place in a good church. Hebrews 13:17 says,

> *"Obey those who rule over you, and be submissive, for they watch out for your souls, as those who must give account. Let them do so with joy and not with grief, for that would be unprofitable for you."*

I am a pastor and I realize that one day I am going to stand before God and give an account to Him for the people who attended this church. Did we pray for them? Did we teach them the Word of God? Were we a good example to them? The Bible says there are those such as a pastor who *"rule over you."* That does *not* mean one who controls you, but one who teaches and shows you how to lead a life that is pleasing to God.

BELONGING TO A BODY OF BELIEVERS

I encourage you to find and join a good church. A good church is one that worships God in a Biblical way. It is a place where the teaching and preaching comes from the Bible, not from Reader's Digest. Take time to prayerfully become

> A good church is one where the teaching and preaching comes from the Bible, not from Reader's Digest.

a part of a church where your faith will be strengthened and you will be cared for spiritually so you can continue to grow. Don't just go there. Get involved in building good relationships and serving others.

Chapter 7

MONEY

YOUR NEW LIFE

Your money represents your life. Each week you trade 40-60 hours of your best time, energy, ability, ideas, and relationship for money. That money is a part of your life in a tangible form that you can use to get the goods

Because money can get you so many things, it is the number one false god.

and services you desire. Because money can get you so many things, it is the number one false god. Jesus said,

> *"No one can serve two masters; for either he will hate the one and love the other, or else he will be loyal to the one and despise the other. You cannot serve God and mammon."*

(*"Mammon"* is money and the things money can buy.)

1 Timothy 6:10 says,

> *"For the love of money is a root of all kinds of evil, for which some have strayed from the faith in their greediness, and pierced themselves through with many sorrows."*

It is not money that is evil, but the *love* of money that is. Money itself has no desire or ambitions. If you were to find a bag of money from a drug deal, you would not suddenly have a desire to find a crack house just because it was drug money. No! Money simply allows you to do what is already in your heart. The more money you have, the more you can do what is in your heart. If you trust your money more than you do God, then money is a problem because your trust is in the wrong place.

God's plan to set us free from the love of money is the tithe. Leviticus 27:30 says, *"and all the tithe of the land, whether of the seed of the land or of the fruit of the tree, is the Lord's. It is holy to the Lord."* The tithe is the first dime of every dollar you make, and God says it is His, which makes it holy. (*"Holy"* means "set aside for a special use.")

God has a plan for the first ten percent of each dollar. He wants it to be used for His work—feeding the hungry, helping a missionary, ministering to the youth, even paying a light bill at church. When you bring your tithe to the Lord, you are worshiping Him as you give it. Give it cheerfully. This tells God that His plan for the tithe is more important to you than what you would do with it if you kept it. Actually, the tithe is a way God has provided for you to reaffirm Jesus as Lord of your life and to place your trust in Him to care for you. As a result of your choice to trust Him as your Lord and Provider, God promises to bless you:

"Honor the Lord with your possessions, and with the first fruits of all your increase; so your barns will be filled with plenty, and your vats will overflow with new wine" (Proverbs 3:9-10).

He also promises,

"Give, and it will be given to you: good measure, pressed down, shaken together, and running over will be put into your bosom. For with the same measure that you use, it will be measured back to you" (Luke 6:38).

In 28 years of being a tithing Christian, I believe it has never cost me anything because God has always blessed and given back far more than I gave in the tithe. He has thousands of ways to bless, and not every blessing involves money. He also gives peace, health, joy and much, much more. I believe that after taking out the first ten percent for the tithe, we always live better on the remaining 90 percent with God's blessing than when we try to live on 100 percent without His blessing.

God also tells us where to bring the tithe.

"'Bring all the tithes into the storehouse, that there may be food in My house, and try Me now in this,' says the Lord

of hosts, 'if I will not open for you the windows of heaven and pour out for you such blessing that there will not be room enough to receive it'" (Malachi 3:10).

The storehouse is the local church where you are fed spiritually and cared for. God says your faithfulness in tithing will enable Him to open the windows of Heaven and pour out blessings on your life.

2 Corinthians 9:6-8 (LB) explains it this way,

". . .if you give little, you will get little. A farmer who plants just a few seeds will get only a small crop, but if he plants much, he will reap much. Everyone must make up his own mind as to how much he should give. Don't force anyone to give more than he really wants to, for cheerful givers are the ones God prizes. God is able to make it up to you by giving you everything you need and more, so that there will not only be enough for your own needs, but plenty left over to give joyfully to others."

Chapter 8

CONFESSING
YOUR SINS

YOUR NEW LIFE

Sometimes people think Christians are never supposed to make a mistake or do anything wrong. That is not true or the Bible wouldn't tell Christians what they should do when they sin. 1 John 1:9 says, *"If we confess our sins, He is faithful and just to forgive us our sins and to cleanse us from all unrighteousness."* Confessing our sin is different than confessing Jesus as our Lord and turning our back on our old life. The Bible calls that repentance—turning and going in a different direction. That's what it takes to get saved. But once we are saved, there will be times when we will sin. God tells us to confess that sin: "God, I did this . . . I had these wrong thoughts. I need the blood of Jesus to cleanse me from this unrighteousness." The Bible says God will hear and forgive us.

What about unconfessed sin? Unconfessed sin in our hearts does two things. First, it hardens our heart toward God so we are no longer responsive to His Spirit and our fellowship with God is broken. Second, it gives that unconfessed sin a chance to take root in our lives. That's why it is important to confess sin and receive forgiveness and cleansing right away.

Once you confess your sin and ask forgiveness, the sin is gone. The Bible says, *"Their sins and their iniquities I will remember no more"* (Hebrews 8:12, KJV).

Once you confess your sin and ask forgiveness, the sin is gone.

That means, as far as God is concerned, that sin

46

never took place. However, Satan will try to make you think God is still mad at you and will not bless, heal, or use you. He tries to condemn you because of past sins. But Romans 8:1 says,

> *"There is therefore now no condemnation to those who are in Christ Jesus, who do not walk according to the flesh, but according to the Spirit."*

When you confess your sin, it is immediately forgiven; and in God's eyes, it's as though you never sinned. The Bible calls this being "justified"—just as if I'd never sinned. What an incredible, loving gift! God wants you to know that *"He made Him who knew no sin to be sin for us, that we might become the righteousness of God in Him* [Jesus]*"* (2 Corinthians 5:21). God takes your sin and puts it on Jesus at the cross, then takes Jesus' righteousness and gives it to you. What an exchange! Why take the devil's gift of condemnation when God is offering you a gift of righteousness?

Neither does God want you to have a shameful consciousness of your past. He doesn't want you to think of yourself as a liar, a drug addict, or an adulterer. Hebrews 9:14 says,

> *"how much more shall the blood of Christ, who through the eternal Spirit offered Himself without spot to God,*

cleanse your conscience from dead works to serve the living God?"

Without a clean conscience you will not be able to serve God the way you should. The blood cleanses even your conscience. When you think of yourself, you need to think of yourself as a child of God, forgiven, a new person in Christ Jesus whose past is gone. You are now made righteous. That's the way God sees you, and that's the way you need to see yourself.

> The blood cleanses even your conscience.

Chapter 9

PRAYER

Prayer is simply talking to God. Sometimes we try to look for prewritten prayers or certain formulas, but what God really desires in prayer is a relationship with you. Relationship doesn't come by a formula, but by pouring out your heart to Him.

Prayer has many important aspects. One is simply talking to God, bringing your petitions to Him and talking all your concerns over with Him. After all, Jesus came so we could have that kind of relationship with God.

Another important aspect of prayer is praying in Jesus' name. Jesus said, *"Whatever you ask the Father in My name He will give you"* (John 16:23). Jesus gave us His name to use. When we use Jesus' name, it's as if Jesus Himself was making the request. The Bible tells us, *"Let us then approach the throne of grace with confidence, so that we may receive mercy and find grace to help us in our time of need."* We can come with confidence because we're coming in Jesus' name.

> *Relationship doesn't come by a formula, but by pouring out your heart to Him.*

We also need to come with a grateful heart. Giving thanks is the protocol for entering the presence of God. Psalms 100:4 says, *"Enter into His gates with thanksgiving and into His courts with praise. Be thankful to Him and bless His name."* This is not a formula. This is an attitude of our hearts. Thanking God reminds us of our dependence on Him. Not only that, but something else very important happens when we express our thankfulness to Him. In Psalms 69:30 David explains what happens: *"I will praise the name of God with a song, and will <u>magnify Him with thanksgiving</u>."* Thankfulness opens our eyes to see how big He really is, how much He really loves us and wants to move in our lives. Beginning our prayers with thanksgiving is very important. Our problems get small and we see God bigger and bigger as we are thankful.

> *Thankfulness opens our eyes to see how big He really is, how much He really loves us and wants to move in our lives.*

Part of prayer is talking to God; the other part is listening to Him. God wants to speak to you. He usually does this through His Word, but He also speaks through desires. Philippians 2:13 (TNT) says, *"God himself is at work in you, inspiring you to want those things which please him and to work for them."* When God directs you to do something, He will give you peace inside to do it. If He doesn't want you to do it, He will remove that peace. Colossians 3:15 puts it this way, *"Let the peace of God rule in your hearts."* Another translation (WT) says, *". . . may it* [peace] *be the umpire in making all your decisions."* Part of your prayer is talking to Him, but don't forget to listen.

There are some things God invites you to ask

for in prayer. One of those things is wisdom. James 1:5 says, *"If any of you lacks wisdom, let him ask of God, who gives to all liberally and without reproach, and it will be given to him."* He also invites us to confess our sins in prayer. *"If we confess our sins, He is faithful and just to forgive us our sins and to cleanse us from all unrighteousness"* (1 John 1:9). He also tells us *"whenever you stand praying, if you have anything against anyone, forgive him, that your Father in heaven may also forgive you your trespasses"* (Mark 11:25). You will find more on this in the next chapter. God doesn't want us to worry about the cares of this life. He wants us to talk everything over with Him. *"Be anxious for nothing,"* He says. He tells us in

> *You have a special invitation from God to talk to Him about everything.*

Philippians 4:6, *"but in everything by prayer and supplication, with thanksgiving, let your requests be made known to God."* As you grow in your new life in Christ, remember that you have a special invitation from God to talk to Him about everything. He *wants* to meet your needs and to build a relationship with you. Take time to pray every day!

Chapter 10

FORGIVENESS

YOUR NEW LIFE

Forgiveness doesn't take a lot of time; but too often *deciding* to forgive does. Forgiving others, however, should never be put off.

> *"And whenever you stand praying* [that is, *anytime* you pray!], *if you have anything against anyone, forgive him, that your Father in heaven may also forgive you your trespasses."*
>
> (Mark 11:25).

Jesus makes two all-inclusive statements when He says, *"if you have anything against anyone."* No matter what anyone has done to you, no matter who they are—and often they're the persons closest to you such as a wife, husband, father, mother or best friend—Jesus says you need to forgive. Sometimes you might feel it is just one little thing that you have against someone. Jesus didn't say if you have *many* things against someone; He said if you *any* thing, even little irritations, when you stand praying you must forgive.

Make the deliberate decision to forgive and release that person. Forgiveness is a decision to stop demanding any payment, any recompense for the wrong done to you. Forgive them and ask God to forgive you for having harbored unforgiveness.

Forgiveness is a decision to stop demanding any payment, any recompense for the wrong done to you.

If you don't forgive, you are giving Satan an opportunity to invade your life. *"Be angry, and do not sin; do not let the sun go down on your wrath, nor give place to the devil"* (Ephesians 4:26-27). Anger is an emotion we all have to deal with. Anger becomes a sin when we let the day go by without forgiving the person who wronged us. The day's leftover anger turns into wrath or "hot anger." That is what gives the devil a place in our lives.

Saul found out about leftover anger the hard way. This story from 1 Samuel 17 and 18 tells what happened after David killed the Philistine's hero, Goliath. When the Israelite army came back after the great victory, the women came out to meet King Saul with tambourines, with joy and musical instruments. Their victory song gave more honor to David than to King Saul. Saul was so angry and jealous that he began to suspect David of wanting his kingdom. The *next day* (see 1 Samuel 18:10) an evil, distressing spirit came upon Saul, and he began to look for ways to kill David.

When Saul refused to forgive, he became bitter and the next day a distressing or evil spirit came. When you do not forgive, you invite Satan to come into your life. Hebrews 12:15 says,

"Looking diligently lest anyone fall short of the grace of God; lest any root

*of bitterness springing up cause trouble,
and by this many become defiled."*

Anger and unforgiveness can ruin our life
as well as the lives of those around us. We
think we can focus our anger like a laser beam
against a certain person, but anger is like a
hydrogen bomb that explodes causing all kinds
of collateral damage to those around us. No
wonder Ecclesiastes 7:9 says, *"Do not hasten in
your spirit to be angry."*

This same scripture also adds, *"Anger rests
in the bosom of fools."* There are people around
you who look good outwardly, but inwardly
they are ready to explode with built up anger
from unresolved conflicts. They think they
can focus their anger on the one who wronged
them. But the truth is, they can't. That anger
explodes towards everyone—usually the people
they love the most or work with or are closest to.
Bitterness, anger, and hatred are luxuries that
neither you nor I can afford. When someone
does you wrong, forgive right away!

God tells us *how* to forgive in Ephesians 4:32:
*"And be kind to one another, tenderhearted,
forgiving one another, just as God in Christ
forgave you."* When God forgives us, He forgets
and doesn't bring it up again. We need to do the
same thing. Forgiveness is not an emotion; it
is a decision. Yet it is actually more than that.
It is a decision we make *by faith*. According

to the Bible, faith without works is dead. So if we forgive by faith, we also need works. That means praying for them every day. As you do that, something supernatural happens inside of you over the course of time. Your heart begins to turn toward the one you pray for and the One you pray to. God begins to bless them. He will even send people into their life who will share the gospel with them. As you continue to pray, you will notice your feelings toward them are changing.

Joseph is a good example of this. If anyone had reason to be angry, it was Joseph. His jealous brothers hated him so much they threw him in a pit, and then sold him as a slave to some Ishmaelite traders who took him down to Egypt. There a high-ranking official named Potiphar bought him. Potiphar's wife tried to seduce him but failed. So she lied about him and Potiphar threw him into prison. In spite of all this, Joseph kept forgiving, and some years later he was promoted to Prime Minister of all Egypt. When his first son was born, he named him Manasseh, which means "forgetting" because, *"God has caused me to forget all the trouble I have had"* (Genesis 41:51, NIV).

> When you forgive you release the past—not the memory of it, but the pain of it.

The same thing happens when you forgive. You release the past—not the memory of it, but the pain of it.

YOUR NEW LIFE

Joseph also had a second son named Ephraim, which means "doubly fruitful." To be fruitful, you must forgive those who have hurt you. Once you have forgiven, you will become fruitful. Your past will no longer have any effect on your todays or tomorrows.

Chapter 11

THE KINGDOM OF GOD

YOUR NEW LIFE

Jesus talked more about the kingdom of God than any other subject. In fact, He began His ministry with the message, *"The kingdom of God is at hand"* (Mark 1:15). The truth is that Christianity is not a religion, a moral teaching or a philosophy. It is a kingdom.

Christianity is not *like* a kingdom. It *is* a kingdom. Today, it is a spiritual kingdom with Jesus reigning and ruling in our hearts, but the time will come when He will return and rule an earthly kingdom.

Christianity is not like a kingdom. It is a kingdom.

- Revelation 19:15 tells us, *"And He Himself will rule them with a rod of iron."*

- Revelation 11:15 says, *"Then the seventh angel sounded: And there were loud voices in heaven, saying, 'The kingdoms of this world have become the kingdoms of our Lord and of His Christ, and He shall reign forever and ever!'"*

When you became a Christian, God translated you into His kingdom in the realm of the spirit. Colossians 1:13 says,

"[The Father] has delivered and drawn us to Himself out of the control and the dominion of darkness and has

transferred us into the kingdom of the Son of His love" (AMP).

God wants us to think of ourselves as in this world but not part of this world's system or its moral values, concepts, and philosophies. Rather, we are a part of God's kingdom in the earth, and we are to bring that kingdom everywhere we go. When Jesus sent out the seventy, He said,

> *"Whatever city you enter, and they receive you, eat such things as are set before you. And heal the sick there, and say to them, 'The kingdom of God has come near to you'"*
>
> (Luke 10:8-9).

Wherever you go, you are a part of the kingdom of God.

The mystery of the kingdom of God is that it is here, but it is also coming. It is here today in the hearts and lives of followers of Jesus Christ. It will come in its fullness when Jesus returns. We can see this in the prayer that Jesus taught His disciples to pray. This prayer, commonly known as the Lord's Prayer, says: *"Your kingdom come. Your will be done on earth as it is in heaven"* (Matt 6:10).

When Jesus returns and establishes His earthly kingdom, we will see this prayer fulfilled. Until then, you are a part of the kingdom of

God and an ambassador of the kingdom. Paul wrote,

> *"We are Christ's ambassadors, and God is using us to speak to you. We urge you, as though Christ himself were here pleading with you, 'Be reconciled to God'"*
>
> (2 Corinthians 5:20 NLT).

Remember the kingdom of God is here in your heart, and you and I are to bring the kingdom everywhere we go.

Chapter 12

ORTHOPRAXY-
DOING WHAT
YOU BELIEVE

YOUR NEW LIFE

God never intended for Christians to be "so heavenly minded that they are no earthly good." That phrase describes people who are always reading and talking about spiritual things but not applying spiritual principles to their daily lives. In other words, what they are *saying* does not line up with what they are *doing*. They are merely talking the talk.

That's not to say that it isn't important to have your facts straight about God and His ways. That's what *orthodoxy* is. The Greek word *ortho* means correct or straight (for example, an orthopedic surgeon corrects problems with your bones). *Dox* comes from the Greek word for thinking. To have sound orthodoxy, we need to think correctly about God. Studying God's Word, the Bible, helps us do just that. Remember, as I mentioned in chapter 5, we meditate on God's Word *"day and night,"* so we can *"do according to all that is written in it"* (Joshua 1:8).

That's what the Christian life is truly about— *doing* what God said. In other words, you need to put some *orthopraxy* behind your *orthodoxy*. The Greek word *praxis* means action, or more specifically putting your beliefs into practice.

> The Christian life is about putting your beliefs into practice and living a lifestyle that reflects your relationship with God.

So the word *orthopraxy* means correct living. *Orthopraxy* is about putting your beliefs into practice and living a lifestyle that reflects your relationship with God. Anyone can learn how to talk the talk and sound super-spiritual, but what Jesus wants is for us to walk the walk. We do not want to be like the Pharisees of Jesus' day who *knew* all the right things—but weren't *doing* the right things.

When Jesus walked the earth, He was a Man of action. Yes, He taught about the kingdom of God, but He didn't teach just to give us information. He applied kingdom principles to everything He did. He demonstrated how we can live productive, fulfilled lives that make a difference in this world and the next.

John wrote in his Gospel,

> *"And there are also many other things that Jesus did, which if they were written one by one, I suppose that even the world itself could not contain the books that would be written"* (John 21:25).

Can you imagine that? Jesus was such a man of action that there wouldn't be enough room in the whole world to contain a written account of everything He *did!* Think about how He saved you. You were not saved by a philosophy or a religious idea; you were saved by Jesus' actions. He came as a real baby born in a real manger to a real woman. He suffered a real crucifixion with real nails driven through His flesh into a real cross. He really was buried, and on the third day He really rose again. It took real action on His part to save you—that's what He came to *do*, not just to preach about it.

Likewise, walking out our Christianity in the real world takes real action on our part. We cannot confine it to the few hours we spend in church each week or the time we spend reading the Bible each day. That's not how it works.

Living for God's kingdom means laying down your life. You forgive when you're wronged, you love your spouse (lovable or not), work hard for your employer, serve your church, fast, pray, give, and have compassion for the poor, the lost, and the broken. You don't live by feelings or experiences. You walk out your Christianity 24/7 and build your life on the Rock, not the sand.

Sounds like hard work, doesn't it? Think about laying your towel on the sand at the beach. The sand is nice and comfortable; it conforms to your shape. When you get up, your imprint remains. If you lay your towel on a rock, though, when you get up, you're dented. You conform to the shape of the rock, it doesn't conform to you. Rock is solid and immoveable, so wise builders build their house upon the rock, not the sand.

Jesus talked about that in Luke 6:47–49:

"Whoever comes to Me, and hears My sayings and does them, I will show

you whom he is like: He is like a man building a house, who dug deep and laid the foundation on the rock. And when the flood arose, the stream beat vehemently against that house, and could not shake it, for it was founded on the rock. But he who heard and did nothing is like a man who built a house on the earth without a foundation, against which the stream beat vehemently; and immediately it fell. And the ruin of that house was great."

Jesus was saying that to build a solid Christian walk, we need to both hear *and* do what He says. We need to add *orthopraxy* to our *orthodoxy* and combine right living with right thinking. As I said earlier, orthodoxy certainly has its place. Psalm 119:15 (NLT) says, *"I will study your commandments and reflect on your ways."* Continually understanding more about God's ways is vital—but don't stop there.

If you ever attended Sunday School as a child, you may remember singing, "This little light of mine, I'm gonna let it shine." It is a cute children's song, but one that should challenge believers of all ages. Jesus said,

"You are the light of the world. A city that is set on a hill cannot be hidden. Nor do they light a lamp and put it under a

basket, but on a lamp stand, and it gives light to all who are in the house. Let your light so shine before men, that they may see your good works and glorify your Father in heaven"

(Matthew 5:14-16).

God's message is plain; believers are called to unashamedly live a life for Jesus that gives light to others. Anything less is as ineffective as hiding a light under a basket.

Our lives should declare to the world what God's grace has done. We should not merely blend in with the rest of the culture. The Apostle Peter advocated living a counter-cultural lifestyle. He said,

"Dear friends, I urge you, as aliens and strangers in the world, to abstain from sinful desires, which war against your soul. Live such good lives among the pagans that, though they accuse you of doing wrong, they may see your good deeds and glorify God..."

(1 Peter 2:11-12).

Your witness in word and deed is vital to others coming to Christ, but even the brightest light does no good when it is hidden. While none of us would actually put a light under a basket, we do sometimes hide our light.

ORTHOPRAXY-DOING WHAT YOU BELIEVE

Your light is hidden if you:

- remain silent when you know you should speak up.
- go along with the crowd.
- live inconsistently.
- say one thing and do another.
- let sin dim your witness.

Your light shines bright when you:

- love God and others - *"You shall love the Lord your God with all your heart, with all your soul, and with all your mind….and… love your neighbor as yourself"* (Matthew 22:37-39).
- renew your mind - *"Do not be conformed to this world, but be transformed by the renewing of your mind, that you may prove what is that good and acceptable and perfect will of God"* (Romans 12:2).
- walk in the Spirit - *"Walk in the Spirit, and you shall not fulfill the lust of the flesh"* (Galatians 5:16).
- are steadfast - *"Be steadfast, immovable, always abounding in the work of the Lord, knowing that your labor is not in vain in the Lord"* (1 Corinthians 15:58).
- do the right thing - *"Even a child is known by his deeds, whether what he does is pure and right"* (Proverbs 20:11).

YOUR NEW LIFE

- live consistently – *"Let us hold fast the confession of our hope without wavering, for He who promised is faithful"* (Hebrew 10:23).

As believers, you and I are simply in the world—physically present—but not of it, not part of its value system. Jesus has placed you in the world to be a light because He is *"not willing that any should perish but that all should come to repentance"* (2 Peter 3:9).

Today, whether young or old, we must let our lights shine in a world that needs to see the love of God in action. That is only going to happen when we live lives that are notably different from unbelievers. You may not always feel like a light. You may even think that you are unprepared to shine. Put those thoughts aside and remember that, as a follower of Jesus, He has already said to you, *"You are the light of the world."*

So now, go out and live your new life…and shine!

Dear God,

I come in Jesus' Name. I believe that Jesus is Your Son, that He died on the cross and shed His precious blood to pay for my sins. I receive your forgiveness for all my sins. I believe Jesus rose again so I make Him the Lord of my life. I am not going to live to please myself any longer. I'm going to live for Jesus every day. Thank you that I'm forgiven, I'm saved, and I'm on my way to Heaven.

In Jesus' Name, Amen.

ABOUT THE AUTHOR

Duane G. Vander Klok

Pastor Duane and Jeanie Vander Klok are the lead pastors of Resurrection Life Church of Grandville, Michigan. Resurrection Life Church has a weekly attendance of over 8,000. The Vander Kloks served for seven years in Mexico with an emphasis on church planting and teaching in Bible schools.

Presently Pastor Duane travels in the United States and abroad encouraging the Body of Christ with practical teaching from the Word of God. He gives oversight to many churches in Michigan and hosts a daily television program called "Walking by Faith."

The Vander Klok family includes three sons and one daughter, their spouses, and grandchildren.

If you have a need in your life and you would like us to agree with you in prayer, please call the Walking by Faith prayer line at 1-800-988-5120.

If you would like additional copies of this book or other resources by Pastor Duane Vander Klok, please contact the Word Shop Bookstore at Resurrection Life Church by calling (616) 249-3724. You can also shop online at www.walkingbyfaith.tv.

Your heart is like a trunk—a suitcase you carry with you throughout your life. And without a doubt, nothing can hinder your spiritual growth as much as letting a little unforgiveness into your trunk. Its poison soon seeps into your relationships with God, family, and friends—and will eventually destroy you.

In *Get the Junk Out of Your Trunk*, Pastor Duane Vander Klok shows you how to recognize unforgiveness in your life, and he reveals how Scripture can help you clean out your trunk for good. In doing so, you will make room for the peace and victory God wants you to experience daily.

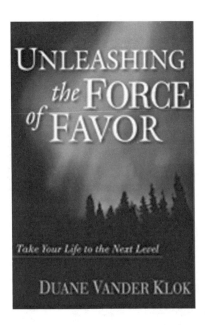

Favor is the "I'm-for-you!" attitude of God toward you. It is an undeserved, amazing benefit of being His child. But because many of us misunderstand the force of God's favor, we live without it.

You may feel that God's favor is absent in your life because He is withholding it. You may think you have to talk God into releasing it. But God's mighty favor is already freely given to us all!

Through biblical examples and powerful personal experience, Pastor Duane will help you realize that God means for you to enjoy His favor every day. Duane offers practical, scriptural advice on the importance of raising your expectation of favor, believing God's promises about it and letting your faith move your mouth, so you can unleash the force of favor in your life.

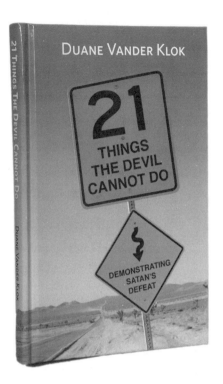

Satan is a defeated foe. Jesus came that He might "destroy the works of the devil" (1 John 3:8), and He did just that. Our job is to demonstrate Satan's defeat in our daily lives and take ground for the Kingdom of God.

"Know your enemy" is an ancient military principle that has stood the test of time, and nowhere is it more applicable than in spiritual warfare. In the midst of battle, it is important to know that the devil's weaknesses far outnumber his strengths.

Knowing all the things the devil cannot do equips us to take a firm grip on the mighty spiritual weapons Jesus gave us and wield them more effectively to secure victory over the kingdom of darkness. With Jesus the Deliverer leading us in triumph, we can show Satan how it's going to be… $12.99

DEALING WITH

Death

*Biblical Answers to
Questions You Weren't
Ready to Ask*

Duane Vander Klok

Death is an inevitable event. No other experience in life can affect us so deeply. If you have ever experienced the death of a loved one, you know the many questions that churn through one's mind. Why? Where is he? If only... Then other unavoidable questions arise demanding immediate answers. What now? Whom do we call first?

What kind of burial arrangements should we make? In His Word, God provides the answers to those questions we weren't ready to ask. I trust His Word will comfort, encourage, and strengthen you.

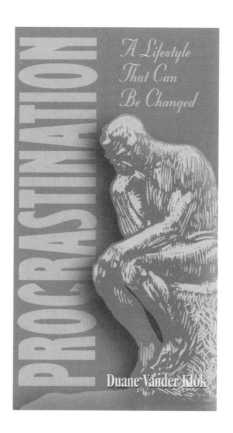

Do you procrastinate?

Do you start projects and never finish them?

Do you start a diet but never carry it past a week?

Do you have the Some Day syndrome?

If you see your God-given potential for success deteriorating into a rash of Some days—"Some day I'll deal with that problem; some day I'll get the training I need; one of these days I'll fix that broken door;"—you are a procrastinator.

The procrastination lifestyle robs you of much more than earthly success…it will affect your eternal rewards.

REVERSING THE DEVIL'S DECISIONS

Duane Vander Klok

God has a plan for you, and Satan has a plan for you. God's plan is for abundant living. Satan's plan is for abundant misery.

Because of God's tremendous love for you, He does not leave you at the devil's mercy. He still has a plan for you and He never intended for you to fulfill Satan's plan.

Your tomorrow is determined by whose plan you choose today! What the devil decides to do to you can be reversed . . . choose God's plan of abundance.

How to Kill a
GIANT

Duane Vander Klok

Like sneering giants, problems can loom over you, haunt you, and make situations seem hopeless. As a believer in Jesus Christ, you are neither hopeless nor helpless!

God is bigger than any giant you will ever face, and He always wins. Whether your giant is failure, divorce, suicide, or bankruptcy, it is small in comparison to God. Even if all your family members for decades past have been alcoholics, abusive parents, or addicts, you can be different. You can wage war on your giants and win.

With God all things are possible. You can be a giant killer!

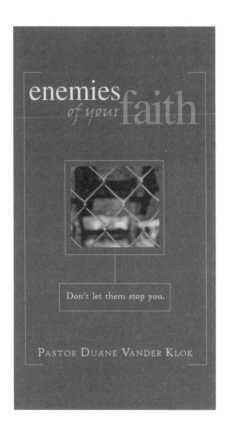

enemies *of your* faith

Don't let them stop you.

PASTOR DUANE VANDER KLOK

Don't let them stop you!

Enemies of your Faith by Pastor Duane Vander Klok is designed to help you have a strong, productive faith in God. While Satan's goal is to steal God's Word from your heart and paralyze your faith, you don't have to let him. This series will help you recognize and defeat enemies of your faith including hardness of heart, condemnation, worry, the traditions of men, and more.

BAPTISM
in the
HOLY
SPIRIT

DUANE VANDER KLOK

Salvation is just the beginning of a wonderful new life! Through salvation God has made His gifts and promises available to every believer. One of the most precious gifts of all is the gift of the Holy Spirit. At the moment of salvation, the Holy Spirit gives us a new heart and new nature. But God wants to do more than that. He wants to transform us into unshakeable, victorious people through whom He can pour out His love, power, and blessings to others. That's what the baptism in the Holy Spirit is all about.